fashion
sourcebooks

The 1930s

John Peacock

Fashion Sourcebooks The 1930s

With 281 illustrations

Thames and Hudson

For Janet Powell

© 1997 Thames and Hudson Ltd,
London

British Library Cataloguing-
in-Publication Data
A catalogue record for this book is
available from the British Library.

ISBN 0-500-27973-X

Printed and bound in Slovenia by
Mladinska Knjiga

Contents

Introduction

The holiday mood of the hectic and emancipated 1920s, with its dramatic rejection of womanly curves and feminine flounces, faded with the dawn of the 1930s, a decade plagued by worldwide economic depression.

The fashionable clothes of the previous period, which had been drawn with bold outlines, no waist, abbreviated hemlines and a denial of feminine curves, gave way to a longer, leaner and more figure-hugging silhouette which defined the waist, accentuated the shoulders and narrowed the hips. The fashionable thirties woman emerged mature, understated, cautious and, above all, sophisticated. Her wardrobe contained specialist outfits for every occasion: day, afternoon, sport, spectator sport, informal evening, formal evening, dinner, theatre and more.

Until the middle of the decade, women's fashion moved comparatively slowly. By 1935 the look which had emerged was epitomized by the suit, either crisply tailored or more softly structured. A sleek, fitted jacket, with square, padded shoulders and a tiny waist in its proper place, was teamed with a skirt or dress in matching fabric. This outfit was considered the ultimate in elegance and chic.

The introduction of washable, easy-care luxury fabrics, such as silk, crepe-de-chine and satin, revolutionized garments of all kinds, from nightdresses to underwear to day dresses and blouses. In addition, the development of man-made fabrics, such as rayon, viscose rayon and tricot, and the improved methods of manufacturing and mass-production techniques meant that well-made and well-cut clothes became available to a wider range of women.

From 1930 evening dresses were a fashion unto themselves. Long or ankle-length, often with a short train, they were moulded onto the body like wet cloth by means of bias-cutting. As much flesh as possible was revealed: for example, halter necklines left the shoulders and most of the back exposed. As the decade progressed, evening dresses became increasingly more extravagant and varied in style, ranging from sleek and figure-hugging crepes and silk satins, to ruffled diaphanous silk-organdie dresses with puffed sleeves, to multi-layered embroidered net crinolines with tightly fitted, boned, strapless bodices.

Fur – both of the expensive and the cheap varieties – was worn extensively throughout the 1930s in the form of coats, capes, stoles, wraps, accessories and trimmings. The most popular furs were sable, mink, chinchilla, Persian lamb and silver fox, all worn both for day and evening.

As far as men's fashions were concerned, developments in style, colour and cut were extremely slow and, in consequence, they require fewer illustrations. The minor differences which do occur in the basic trends have been shown, on average, with one example for each page.

In the main, the fashions I have illustrated are such as would have been worn by the middle or upper-middle classes and by people who, while not being 'dedicated followers of fashion', would have had a keen interest in the latest styles.

The sources from which I have drawn – chiefly from Great Britain, North America and France – include contemporary magazines, journals and catalogues, museum collections, original photographs, and my own costume collection.

This sourcebook is divided into ten sections, each of which includes four subdivisions covering Day Wear, Evening Wear (alternately, on two occasions, Wedding Wear), Sports and Leisure Wear and a section on either Underwear or Accessories. Following the main illustrations are ten pages of schematic drawings accompanied by detailed notes about each example, giving particulars of colour, fabric, cut and trimming as well as other useful information. Then follow two pages of drawings which illustrate the decade 'at a glance' and which demonstrate the evolution of the period and its main development trends.

Biographies of the most important fashion designers of the decade are also included as well as a list of further reading suggestions into the styles of this period.

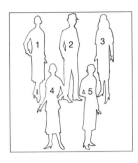

1930 Day Wear

1 Fine cream silk dress spotted in pale orange, low round neckline, brown satin roll collar, ends tied into bow, matching cuffs of long fitted inset sleeves and narrow buckled belt, semi-fitted bodice, top-stitched bolero effect, repeated in hip-level seaming of bias-cut mid-calf-length skirt. Brown leather shoes, bow trim, pointed toes, high heels. **2** Three-piece light-brown wool suit: single-breasted jacket, two-button fastening, flap pockets; single-breasted collarless waistcoat; straight-cut trousers with turn-ups. White cotton collar-attached shirt. Brown and black spotted silk tie. Light-brown trilby. Brown lace-up shoes.
3 Brown and beige wool-tweed two-piece suit: single-breasted knee-length coat, long roll collar, wide fur trim at neck, short shoulder cape, long inset sleeves trimmed with brown velvet L-shaped cuffs, button detail, line repeated as side panels in skirts and incorporates pockets; straight skirt. Fitted brown velvet brimless hat, gathered and buttoned on one side. Brown gloves. Brown leather shoes, elasticated front panels. **4** Dark-red wool-crepe dress, semi-fitted bodice, low neckline, roll collar held in place by self-fabric strap buttoned onto short shoulder cape and at waist above bow-trimmed belt, trim repeated on frilled cuffs of long fitted inset sleeves, bias-cut skirt, curved side panel seams with circular-cut sheet floating panels on side hips. Black leather shoes.
5 Mid-blue, dark-blue and grey flecked wool-jersey dress, asymmetric neckline trimmed with navy-blue top-stitched satin matching threaded tie detail under point of neckline, trim above wrists of inset sleeves, narrow belt and covered buckle, asymmetric hip yoke, flared skirt, pleated side panel. Fitted brimless hat, scalloped edges, matching dress fabric. Navy-blue leather shoes, buckle trim.

Evening Wear

1 Leaf-brown silk-chiffon dinner dress, low boat-shaped neckline, semi-fitted sleeveless bodice, brown velvet ribbon belt with jeweled buckle, bias-cut skirt, deep asymmetric hip yoke, two tiers of circular frills following line through to hem, brown crepe-de-chine underslip, semi-fitted bodice, narrow shoulder straps, bias-cut skirt. Brown satin shoes, pointed toes, high heels. **2** Burnt-orange velvet-embossed georgette evening dress, low scooped neckline, short circular-cut sleeves, bias-cut skirt to knee-level, scalloped seam, orange silk fishtail circular hem, matching belt with jeweled buckle, orange chiffon scarf. Silk shoes, bead trim, pointed toes.
3 Three-piece black wool evening suit: jacket with linked-button fastening, wide lapels faced with satin, piped pockets; low-cut single-breasted waistcoat; straight-cut trousers, satin ribbon trim on outside seams, no turn-ups. White shirt worn with wing collar and black satin bow-tie. Black patent-leather shoes.
4 Black silk-chiffon evening dress, low V-shaped neckline, matching line of inserted lace panel in sleeveless, semi-fitted bodice and in side panels of bias-cut ankle-length skirt, large black velvet roses on one shoulder, dress worn over black silk slip of same shape. Black velvet clutch purse. Black silk shoes.
5 Multicoloured net evening dress, wide boat-shaped neckline, narrow cape collar with frilled edge matching two rows of frills above hem of bias-cut skirt, semi-fitted sleeveless bodice, narrow self-fabric belt, jeweled buckle, scalloped hip-level yoke seam. Small silver clutch purse; matching shoes, pointed toes, high heels.

Sports and Leisure Wear

1 Tennis. Sleeveless semi-fitted white cotton blouse, V-shaped neckline, mock collar and revers trimmed with navy-blue ribbon, matching long knotted tie. Flared white linen skirt, narrow waistband, wide unpressed box-pleats either side centre front, top-stitched to above knee-level. White silk stockings. White leather bar-strap shoes.
2 Skating. Fawn wool-stockinette single-breasted jacket, fastening from hip-level to neck with self-fabric-covered buttons, long fitted inset sleeves, piped pockets above self-fabric buttoned belt. Canary-yellow wool-stockinette scarf, blanket-stitched edges; matching gauntlet gloves and brimless hat. Dark-green wool-stockinette bias-cut skirt to below knee-level. Long beige leather laced skating boots and blades. **3** Country wear. Mottled brown, beige and green wool-jersey three-piece suit: long sweater, V-shaped neckline and mock buttoned strap opening to waist-level edged with dark green crepe-de-chine, matching hip-level pockets, trim on sleeves, pockets, edges of edge-to-edge jacket, scarf and band on edge of beret; flared skirt, top-stitched centre-front inverted box-pleat. Two-tone lace-up leather shoes.
4 Golf. Light-brown and tan checked wool three-piece suit: single-breasted jacket, three-button fastening, flap pockets; collarless single-breasted waistcoat; knee-length plus-fours. Collar-attached shirt. Striped wool tie. Long fawn wool socks. Brown leather lace-up brogues. **5** Golf. Cream machine-knitted wool sweater, V-shaped neckline edged in dark green, matching inset bands, wide centre-front buttoned band, cuffs of inset sleeves and hem. Dark-green accordion-pleated wool skirt. Dark-green wool shirt. Tan wool tie. Dark-green wool brimless hat, tan trim. Tan leather gloves; matching shoes.

Underwear and Negligee

1 Pale-peach artificial-silk chemise top, edged with darker peach binding and appliqué leaves, matching ribbon shoulder straps. Peach brocade corset, deep boned and stitched waistband, ribbed elastic side inserts over hips, boned side-front control darts, centre-front hook-and-bar fastening to mid-hip, laced to hem, four adjustable suspenders. Flesh-coloured silk stockings. **2** Yellow artificial-silk chemise top, edged and trimmed with pale green rouleau, matching shoulder straps; knickers in matching fabric and trim, shaped hip yoke, side-button fastening, long legs, narrow cuffs, inside leg button fastening. **3** Black silk-georgette slip, low brassiere top trimmed with fine black lace, matching hem and hems of knicker legs, black satin ribbon shoulder straps. **4** Green, cream and yellow striped cotton pyjamas: single-breasted jacket, four-button fastening to under shirt collar, single breast patch pocket, long inset sleeves, stitched cuffs; straight-cut trousers. Black leather step-in slippers. **5** Pink cotton corselette, wide shaped boned waistband and fitted upper bodice covered in pink lace, satin ribbon shoulder straps, lightly boned front panels, top-stitched seams, elasticated side-hip panels, four adjustable suspenders, side hook-and-bar fastening. Flesh-coloured silk stockings. **6** Sunrise-pink crepe-de-chine nightdress patterned with cream and pale-green flowers, sleeveless semi-fitted bodice, low V-shaped neckline, two bands of crossed écru lace to give bolero effect, ankle-length bias-cut skirt, self-fabric tie-belt. Pale-pink velvet mules, scalloped edges, pointed toes, medium heels.

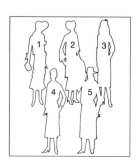
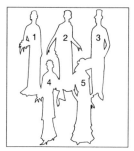
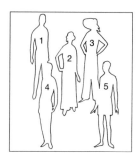

1931 Day Wear

1 Navy-blue wool-georgette dress patterned with large dark-pink flowers, semi-fitted bodice, V-shaped neckline formed by asymmetric wrapover front, edged with circular frill, large bow trim on one side above bust, matching trim above wrists on fitted inset sleeves, self-fabric belt, bias-cut mid-calf-length skirt, low asymmetric hip yoke, three tiers of circular frills. Semi-transparent top-stitched pink silk hat. Navy-blue leather clutch bag; matching shoes. **2** Powder-blue wool-crepe two-piece: edge-to-edge jacket, scalloped hem, matching long flared inset sleeves; dress with semi-fitted bodice, low scooped neckline, white cotton piqué wrapover infill, scalloped edges, self-fabric belt and covered oval buckle, two-tier skirt, scalloped hems. Natural straw hat, pale-blue ribbon band, peach suede flowers. Navy-blue leather clutch bag; matching shoes. Fox-fur stole. **3** Fitted natural-sable hip-length jacket, single fur-covered button-and-loop fastening, high shawl collar, inset sleeves eased into deep cuffs, pelts used vertically, horizontally and diagonally. Cream wool skirt, box-pleats and inverted box-pleats. Tan suede beret. Tan leather shoes. **4** Navy-blue and white wool-crepe dress, low V-shaped neckline faced in white, matching pointed yoke, upper part and pointed cuffs of semi-set-in sleeves, navy-blue covered button detail, pointed scalloped panel above hem of bias-cut skirt, semi-fitted bodice, narrow belt, lower part of sleeves and upper part of skirt all in navy-blue. Navy-blue brimless wool beret. Navy-blue leather shoes. **5** Double-breasted wrapover camel-hair overcoat, wide buckled belt, wide lapels, large collar, inset sleeves, deep cuffs, hip-level welt pockets, top-stitched edges and detail. Straight-cut trousers, turn-ups. Brown trilby. Checked wool scarf. Brown leather gloves and shoes.

Wedding Wear

1 Off-white satin wedding dress, wide scooped neckline edged with pearls, matching hems of fitted full-length inset sleeves, semi-fitted bodice, self-fabric belt, bow trim, long bias-cut skirt gathered from low hip yoke and knee-level seams, short back train. Mid-calf-length silk-tulle veil gathered from self-fabric cap edged with pearls and trimmed with satin roses over each ear. **2** Pale-green satin bridesmaid's dress, sleeveless semi-fitted bodice, decorative curved seam from under arm to centre front, repeated as hip yoke in full-length bias-cut skirt, self-fabric pleated belt, V-shaped neckline, attached self-fabric bias-cut knee-length cape. Tiara of looped ribbon and wax flowers. **3** Morning suit: single-breasted dark-grey wool tailcoat, single-button fastening, double-breasted lapels; single-breasted pale-grey wool collarless waistcoat; black and grey striped trousers, no turn-ups. Light grey top hat. Black shoes worn with grey spats. **4** Oyster crepe-de-chine two-piece: collarless edge-to-edge bolero jacket, inset sleeves, flared cuffs from diagonal seam below elbows; sleeveless dress, semi-fitted bodice, low neckline, self-fabric belt, brooch trim, knee-length overskirt, bias-cut flare from under shaped yoke seam which matches details of ankle-length underskirt. Tiara of silk and wax flowers, full-length silk-tulle veil. Oyster satin shoes, high heels. **5** Turquoise-blue silk-chiffon bridesmaid's dress, semi-fitted bodice, low round neckline, short circular cap sleeves, turquoise and pink chiffon twisted into belt with two-tone bow trim, full-length bias-cut skirt, circular frills at knee, mid-calf and ankle-level. Large pink straw hat, shallow crown, narrow turquoise ribbon band, pink rose trim, wide wired brim. Long pink gloves. Turquoise satin shoes.

Sports and Leisure Wear

1 Swimming. Dark-blue knitted-cotton sleeveless vest, low scooped neckline, open sides, bands of green and red stripes across chest. Fitted green cotton-jersey shorts, self-fabric belt threaded through loops on waistband, metal clip buckle. **2** Beach wear. Sleeveless white cotton blouse, armholes bound in red, matching low V-shaped neckline, scalloped edge of front opening and covered buttons. Red linen trousers, fitted over hips, wide legs, scalloped hems. Brimless white straw hat, wide red ribbon band. **3** Beach wear. Yellow and green spotted linen halter-neck blouse. Yellow linen trousers, fitted over hips, decorative buttoned waistband, side fastening, wide legs flared at hem, two small hip-level triangular-shaped patch pockets in fabric to match blouse. Yellow varnished-straw hat, small crown, yellow and green spotted scarf, outsize brim. **4** Bathing. Navy-blue, pale-blue and fawn flecked wool-jersey costume, armholes and low scooped neckline bound in navy-blue to match buckled belt and inset band on outside seam of fitted legs. Pale-blue rubber bathing cap edged in navy-blue, matching buckled chinstrap. **5** Beach wear. White cotton-jersey vest, low scooped neckline, self-binding, matching armholes, inset red stripe across chest. Red, white and blue striped cotton-canvas shorts, deep waistband, threaded self-fabric buckled belt, wide legs, fly fastening.

Accessories

1 Dark-brown leather clutch bag, orange plastic catch, V-shaped top-stitched tab. **2** Pale-grey leather clutch bag, clasp fastening. **3** Grey moleskin elbow-length shoulder cape combined with sleeveless waistcoat, shawl collar, single-button fastening. Mustard-yellow felt beret, feather trim. Pale-grey suede gauntlet gloves, leather trim. **4** Navy-blue and cream two-tone leather shoes, high heels, almond toes. **5** Cream canvas shoes, tan leather toecaps, matching high heels, laced bar straps and trim. Silver fox-fur stole. Primrose-yellow felt hat, uneven brim, shallow crown, narrow self-fabric band and bow trim. Yellow leather gloves, scalloped frill, bow trim. **6** Long sable stole. Light-brown brimless beret, cream satin-covered button, leaf and rouleau loop trim. **7** Long pink gloves. **8** Brown and cream checked wool-tweed peaked cap. **9** Brown leather brogues, perforated decoration. **10** Brown and white two-tone leather shoes. **11** Grey felt trilby, tall crown, deep dark-grey petersham ribbon band and bow trim, wide brim. **12** Lilac felt hat, asymmetric top-stitched brim, matching self-fabric bow trim. Grey squirrel scarf, uneven ends threaded through self bow trim. **13** Gold kid evening shoes, brocade fronts and covered heels. **14** Silver kid T-strap dance shoes, sandal fronts, open sides, high heels. **15** South American skunk scarf. Close-fitting brimless feather hat in shades of green. **16** Black leather lace-up ankle-boots, cuffs, low heels. **17** Brown velvet evening bag, shiny brown plastic frame and clasp. **18** Gold kid evening bag, gold metal frame, clasp fastening and long chain handle.

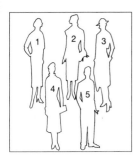

1932 Day Wear

1 Wine-red heavy silk dress, V-shaped neckline meeting point of curved seam running from high waistline at side, matching three seamed panels to hip-level, shaping gathers from shoulder and under bust, long sleeves, full to elbow-level, fitted to wrist, button trim, bias-cut skirt. Dark-red and cream leather shoes, toecaps, high heels. **2** Double-breasted rust coarse-wool-tweed coat, split outsized collar, left side threaded through right forming bow-effect, held by polished-wood button, matching high diagonal three-button fastening at bust level, diagonal elbow-level button trim on long inset sleeves and large round buckle on waist-belt, side hip-level pockets. Small bottle-green felt hat, pointed crown, feather and brooch trim. Bottle-green leather clutch bag, gloves and shoes. **3** Cherry-red ribbed-wool dress, semi-fitted underbodice, horizontal and diagonal rib, double-breasted bolero-effect top, vertical rib matching skirt, large white cotton-piqué lapels, long inset sleeves, horizontal rib, matching narrow belt with round red plastic buckle and curved hip yoke. Red lacquered-straw hat, small pointed crown, white ribbon trim. White cotton gauntlet gloves, red blanket-stitched edges. Fox-fur stole. Red and white leather shoes, toecaps, high heels. **4** Light-brown herringbone weatherproofed wool-tweed coat, double-breasted, two-button fastening, long pointed collar, shaped lapels, button trim, matching detail on long inset sleeves and hip-level pockets. Light-brown knitted-wool beret, brooch trim. Light-brown leather gloves. Brown leather clutch bag; matching shoes. **5** Double-breasted navy-blue wool blazer, wide lapels, flap pockets. Pale-grey flannel trousers, medium-wide legs, turn-ups. White collar-attached shirt. Red and blue striped silk tie. Blue and cream leather lace-up shoes.

Evening Wear

1 Black velvet dinner dress, wide V-shaped neckline, short cape sleeves, padded shoulderline, fitted bodice with asymmetric seaming and gathered shaping, draped and looped self-fabric side-hip detail, long pointed ends, full-length bias-cut flared skirt. Black satin strap sandals. **2** Sleeveless lavender silk-jersey evening dress, low wide V-shaped neckline, curved seam under bust, gathered shaping, bodice gently ruched to hipline, full-length bias-cut flared skirt, asymmetric seam from low side hip to knee level on opposite side, single unpressed knife-pleat and knee-length waterfall on one side. Silver kid strap sandals. **3** Pink silk-organdie dinner dress, asymmetric neckline decorated with self-fabric loops and pointed ends on one side, top-stitched tucks between neckline and short puff sleeves, self-fabric belt, small round self-fabric-covered buckle, full-length bias-cut flared skirt, zig-zag scalloped hip yoke. **4** Heavy black satin-crepe evening dress, wide white piqué shoulder straps, matching large bow trim on side of shaped neckline, self-fabric fitted bodice and full-length flared skirt, pointed seaming under bust, side panel seams pointing to centre front from waist to knee level. **5** Formal dinner dress, beige lace semi-fitted bodice, low-cut back, wide curved V-shaped neckline, attached short shoulder cape, waist-length at back, full-length bias-cut flared skirt in heavy dull-beige silk-crepe.

Sports and Leisure Wear

1 Golf. Hand-knitted bottle-green wool crew-neck sweater and matching collarless cardigan, single-breasted, three-button fastening in deep waist rib, patch pockets, inset sleeves with turned-back cuffs. Green, yellow and brown flecked wool-tweed flared skirt, wide box-pleat buttoned on each side from waist to hip-level, knife-pleat under box-pleat from below button detail to hem. Brimless dark-yellow wool sectioned beret, stalk in centre. Brown and yellow leather shoes, low stacked heels. **2** Holiday wear. Beige cotton dress patterned with brown circles, semi-fitted bodice, cowl neckline, elbow-length circular-cut cape sleeves, draped cummerbund, bias-cut mid-calf-length skirt, asymmetric seaming. Small brimless brown felt hat, cream petersham ribbon bow trim. Beige leather shoes. **3** Tennis. Machine-knitted white cotton shirt, short inset sleeves, buttoned strap opening from chest-level to under collar. White linen trousers, pleats under deep waistband, self-fabric buckled belt, side-hip pockets, wide legs, turn-ups. White leather lace-up shoes. **4** Tennis. Sleeveless white linen dress, semi-fitted bodice, separate apron front, buttoned at bust level, wide stiffened self-fabric belt, asymmetric white plastic buckle, flared panelled mid-calf-length skirt. White leather lace-up shoes, thick medium-high heels. **5** Golf. Hand-knitted maroon wool collarless cardigan, single-breasted, fastening with five leather buttons, inset sleeves, turned-back cuffs, patch pockets above deep welt. Grey and brown flecked wool trousers, side-hip pockets, wide legs, turn-ups. Light-grey wool collar-attached shirt. Striped wool-tweed tie. Two-tone leather lace-up shoes.

Underwear and Negligee

1 Mid-calf-length mustard-yellow quilted-silk dressing gown, wrapover front, black satin roll collar edges piped with yellow silk to match deep cuffs of inset sleeves, tops of hip-level patch pockets and tie-belt with tassel ends. Pale-grey silk pyjamas. Black leather step-in slippers. **2** Pale-peach satin combination camisole and knickers, brassiere top, scalloped edges matching hems of wide legs, button fastening in crotch, narrow self-fabric rouleau shoulder straps. **3** Cream cotton-satin brassiere, fitted cups, adjustable fitting strap from back fastening, narrow adjustable shoulder straps. Lightweight white rubber girdle, high waist, light boning, double front panel, laced side opening, four adjustable suspenders. Pleated pink artificial-silk slip. Dark-flesh silk stockings. **4** Pale-green crepe-de-chine two-piece pyjama suit: short bolero jacket, scalloped edges bound in self-fabric and trimmed with one tiny self-fabric-covered button in each point, full-length sleeves flared from elbow, trimmed with dark-green chiffon and black lace; combination bias-cut top and wide flared trousers, low shaped neckline and seam under bust trimmed to match sleeve hems, wide trousers fall from pointed hip seam and have scalloped hems to match bolero. Pale-green velvet mules trimmed with satin. **5** Pink satin and elastic combination brassiere and girdle, fitted brassiere covered with pink lace, narrow adjustable shoulder straps, hip-length body, elasticated side panels and centre-front gusset, four cotton and elastic adjustable suspenders. Short silk slip. Satin house shoes.

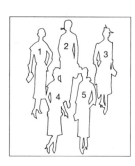

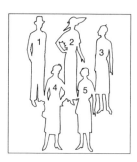

1933 Day Wear

1 Lido-green wool dress, cape collar, scalloped edge bound in black to match half-cuffs of long tight sleeves, belt and covered buckle; semi-fitted bodice, panels extend into flared skirt, brass button trim on diagonal hip seams, matching collar and cuffs. Black felt hat, narrow upturned split brim, self-fabric trim. Black leather clutch bag; matching shoes. 2 Brown and grey checked wool-tweed single-breasted jacket, three-button fastening, patch pockets, inverted box-pleat decoration. Fawn wool trousers, wide legs, turn-ups. Cream collar-attached shirt. Brown wool tie. Fawn trilby. Brown shoes. 3 Slate-blue wool-crepe dress, diagonal fastening to under burnt-orange top-stitched satin collar which matches buttons, belt, round buckle and cuffs set at three-quarter-length on long inset sleeves, gathered heads and padded shoulders, diagonal seam from side waist to opposite side hip, two inverted box-pleats at matching angle on side front of flared skirt. Slate-blue brimless pillbox hat, blue feather trim. Tan leather clutch bag, gloves and shoes. Grey fox fur. 4 Yellow crepe-de-chine dress patterned in brown and dark-red, fitted bodice, round neckline, curved off-the-shoulder yoke edged with narrow frill, repeated in three tiers under low curved hip seam, flared skirt, waist-level slotted belt tied at back, long tight sleeves. Small dark-red felt hat, narrow upturned brim, button trim. Brown leather shoes. 5 Double-breasted wine wool coat, two-button fastening at waist level, inset bias-cut decoration between two vertical panel seams, matching decoration on hip-level pockets, sleeve hems and above trim, inset sleeves with buttoned point extension from elbow. Black felt hat, narrow brim, button trim. Wine and cream striped silk scarf. Black leather clutch bag and shoes.

Evening Wear

1 Black wool two-piece evening suit: double-breasted jacket, wide lapels faced with satin, matching covered buttons, hip-level piped pockets, breast pocket, white silk handkerchief; wide trousers, no turn-ups. White silk shirt worn with wing collar. Black satin bow-tie. Black patent-leather shoes. 2 Pale-gold satin evening dress, low V-shaped neckline and shaped seam under bust to waist-level form upper bodice and shoulder straps, bias-cut bodice and flared skirt with asymmetric seaming. 3 Fine turquoise silk-velvet dance dress, scooped neckline, three-tier self-fabric frilled short cap sleeves, matching frill inserted in shaped seam under bust and four tiers of frills above hem of flared skirt, bias-cut bodice and skirt with shaped seams at hip and knee level. 4 Yellow crepe-de-chine sleeveless dance dress, low wide V-shaped neckline edged with three rows of circular-cut frills of white silk-organdie, black velvet ribbon bow with long ends on centre front, matching cummerbund, semi-fitted bodice, panel seams, repeated in wide flared skirt, circular-cut godets inserted at knee-level of each seam. 5 Dinner outfit: deep-gold satin collarless jacket, wrapover front, tied at back with long waterfall ends, short circular-cut semi-inset sleeves, padded shoulders; black silk-velvet dress, bias-cut fitted bodice and full-length flared skirt, panel seams curving from side-waist to off-centre hip ending in wide flared box-pleat.

Sports and Leisure Wear

1 Country wear. Three-piece brown and beige checked wool suit: single-breasted jacket, two-button fastening, wide lapels, flap pockets; collarless single-breasted waistcoat; wide trousers, turn-ups. White collar-attached shirt. Spotted silk tie. Beige trilby. Brown leather shoes. 2 Racing or garden-party wear. Pink lace two-piece: unlined bolero, scalloped hem, matching elbow-length circular-cut oversleeves, full-length tight undersleeves, button fastening at wrist, long narrow scarf collar; sleeveless dress worn over full-length pink silk petticoat, V-shaped neckline, bodice ruched either side narrow central panel, self-fabric belt, clasp fastening, ankle-length bias-cut flared skirt, scalloped seam at hip-level. Pink straw hat, shallow crown, wide brim. Cream kid shoes. 3 Golf. Three-piece light-brown hand-knitted wool suit: edge-to-edge collarless jacket, buttoned belt, shaped hem, dark-brown cable-knit trim matching hems of long inset sleeves, shaped hem and V-shaped neckline of sleeveless sweater and above hemline of flared skirt. Dark-brown hand-knitted wool hat, rolled brim, stalk trim. Brown and cream leather lace-up shoes, flat heels. 4 Country wear. Two-piece beige and brown flecked wool-tweed suit: single-breasted jacket, two-button fastening, wide lapels, long inset sleeves, padded shoulders, panel seams from shoulders to top of flap pockets; flared panelled skirt. Cream silk blouse, top-stitched stand collar, matching strap opening. Tan felt hat, petersham trim. Tan leather gauntlet gloves and clutch bag. Brown leather lace-up shoes. 5 Tennis. White cotton dress, square neckline, small collar, asymmetric button opening from hip-level through inset waistband to neckline, slightly flared skirt, three knife-pleats on left side. White canvas lace-up shoes, low heels.

Accessories

1 Brown leather clutch bag, decorative stitching, clasp fastening. 2 Brown leather lace-up shoes, piped seams. 3 Red and blue spotted silk beret. Matching scarf tied into large bow. 4 Bottle-green leather clutch bag, tan and cream leather applied trim. 5 Brown leather lace-up shoes, buckled overstrap, perforated trim. 6 Brown and cream leather lace-up shoes. 7 Dusty-pink felt beret, top-stitched pink satin band, self-fabric trim. 8 Blue and beige leather clutch bag, top-stitched trim. 9 Black leather envelope clutch bag, top-stitched flap. 10 Fawn suede lace-up shoes, tan leather heels and trim. 11 Fine pale-yellow straw hat, wide wired brim, shallow crown, satin roses trim. 12 Bottle-green and cream leather shoes, low thick heels. 13 Black satin dance shoes, ankle straps, cut-away sides and front detail, high slender heels. 14 Brown straw hat, tall crown, wide satin band and bow trim, narrow top-stitched brim. 15 Green felt trilby, black petersham band, feather trim. 16 Lace-up tan leather shoes, perforated decoration, low thick heels. 17 Hand-knitted slate-blue beret, bow trim. Matching scarf, double-scalloped hem. 18 Powder-blue felt hat, shallow crown, self-colour petersham band and bow trim, navy-blue and white striped ribbon band, curled brim. Buttoned fur collar. 19 Black straw pillbox hat, black and white ribbon trim on back. 20 Small grey felt hat with turned-up brim, grey ribbon trim. 21 Pink and blue felt gauntlet gloves. 22 Brown leather gauntlet gloves, elasticated at wrist, mock side-button fastening. 23 Hand-knitted cream cotton gauntlet gloves, inset wristband, scalloped edges. 24 Brown and cream leather bar-strap shoes, low stacked heels.

1934 Day Wear

1 Cream and green flecked linen-tweed coat-dress, bloused bodice, front opening from waist to under collar and revers, cream silk infill, long inset sleeves, sewn cuffs, panel seams from padded shoulders to waist, double-breasted button trim, seams continued to hem of flared skirt, self-fabric belt, diamond-shaped brown plastic buckle. Cream felt trilby. Brown leather clutch bag; matching shoes. **2** Double-breasted fawn and donkey-brown herringbone wool-tweed coat, large collar and wide lapels, long inset sleeves with cuffs, padded shoulders, tailored self-fabric buckled belt, narrow skirt, hip-level welt pockets. Brown felt hat, brown and fawn petersham ribbon trim. Orange silk scarf. Fawn suede shoes. **3** Green, red and cream diagonally striped cotton dress, bloused bodice, V-shaped neckline, large self-fabric bow trim, short inset sleeves with cuffs, padded shoulders, flared skirt, green suede belt, large buckle. Green straw hat, wide brim, shallow crown, red and cream petersham ribbon trim. Green leather clutch bag and gauntlet gloves. Brown and cream leather shoes. **4** Three-piece fawn and light-brown striped wool suit: single-breasted jacket, three-button fastening, wide lapels, flap pockets; collarless single-breasted waistcoat; wide trousers, turn-ups. Fawn striped white cotton collar-attached shirt. Brown, red and black patterned silk tie. Fawn felt trilby. Brown leather lace-up shoes. **5** Silver-grey wool-crepe two-piece suit: bloused top, short peplum, V-shaped neckline edged with top-stitched black satin, matching buckled belt, inset sleeves flared and gathered at elbow-level, fitted to wrist, top stitched black satin cuffs, padded shoulders, black and white leather scarf-effect with flared ends buttoned to bodice; bias-cut flared skirt. Black hat. Black and white leather shoes.

Evening Wear

1 Black lace evening dress worn over shell-pink shift of same shape, sleeveless bloused bodice, low scooped neckline draped with bias-cut shell-pink silk-velvet scarf, held on each shoulder by pearl-edged brooch, armholes draped in same fashion, matching velvet belt ruched into pearl-edged buckle, bias-cut skirt, curved V-shaped seam from side hip to centre-front seam, slight train. Wide pink plastic wrist-bangle. **2** Pale-gold silk-satin sleeveless evening dress, boat-shaped neckline draped with self-fabric scarf, ends fall to knee-level at back, hems trimmed with velvet leaves in golds, browns and oranges, matching hem of full-length bias-cut flared skirt, bodice and skirt cut in one piece, asymmetric seaming across body from right shoulder to hem. **3** Moss-green silk-satin sleeveless evening dress, cowl draped from halter-neck, back fastening, fitted bias-cut bodice to four rows of horizontal panels on hipline, curve on side hip and flare into wide panels at hem forming slight train. **4** Black silk-velvet sleeveless evening dress, curved seam under bust from side to centre front, low V-shaped neckline, infilled with bright-red and pink silk roses, matching spray on curved seam at knee-level above deep circular-cut gathered frill, bias-cut fitted bodice and narrow skirt cut in one piece. Large paste wrist-bangle. **5** Jade-green silk-satin sleeveless evening dress, low V-shaped neckline, trimmed on point with large pleated white silk-organdie bow, bias-cut fitted bodice and skirt, intricate seaming under bust, on front bodice and on side hips through to hem, slight train.

Sports and Leisure Wear

1 Holiday wear. Blue, yellow and cream striped cotton jacket, single-breasted two-button fastening, wide lapels, flap pockets. Cream flannel trousers, wide legs, turn-ups, leather belt. Machine-knitted white cotton shirt, short buttoned strap opening to under collar, worn open. Brown leather lace-up shoes. **2** Holiday wear. Pale-blue linen two-piece: fitted blouse top, mock wrapover buttoned fastening, wide shoulder straps, button trim, V-shaped armholes; flared skirt, centre-front box-pleat, hip-level patch pockets, wide waistband, button trim. Blue and yellow checked cotton blouse, short puff sleeves, narrow cuffs, knotted bow trim, matching bow-tie under tiny peter-pan collar. Yellow straw hat, wide brim, shallow crown. Blue and white leather shoes. **3** Holiday wear. White cotton dress patterned in coffee, high round neckline, bound edge, pleated jabot matching short sleeves set into curved yoke seam and hem of straight skirt, bloused bodice, white leather belt buckled over right hip. Brown cotton beret. White cotton gauntlet gloves. Brown leather clutch bag, white trim. Brown leather shoes. **4** Golf. Yellow, brown, beige and orange hand-knitted wool sweater, wide neckline, scarf collar, ends tied at front, long inset sleeves, plain brown turned-back ribbed cuffs, matching deep waistband, above waist to hip-level. Brown and beige wool-tweed flared panelled skirt. Brown knitted-wool beret. Brown leather lace-up shoes, flat heels. **5** Golf. Hand-knitted maroon wool sweater, V-shaped neckline, long inset sleeves, turned-back cuffs. Beige and fawn flecked wool-tweed breeches, legs gathered above knees, side hip pockets. Beige wool collar-attached shirt. Striped wool tie. Beige checked wool-tweed cap. Maroon, cream and fawn checked wool stockings. Brown leather lace-up shoes.

Underwear and Negligee

1 Pale-blue artificial-silk nightdress, bloused bodice trimmed with coffee lace, repeated in V-shaped hip panel and band above hem, tied self-fabric rouleau belt with bow, matching neck edge and shoulder straps. Blue satin mules trimmed with loops of self-fabric rouleau, medium heels. **2** White machine-knitted cotton collarless vest, short sleeves, bound hems to match V-shaped neckline and front opening, rubber buttons. Short white machine-knitted drawers, elasticated waistband, single-button fastening, fly-front opening, V-shaped hip yoke, wide legs, machine-stitched hems. **3** Full-length pale-green crepe-de-chine slip, brassiere top trimmed with fine cream lace and silk ribbon, matching shoulder straps, inverted V-shaped seam from side-waist to centre-front under bust and triangular panels decorating hem of full skirt. **4** Sky-blue combination bodice and pyjama trousers, patterned in bright pink, sleeveless wrapover top, fastening on side left hip, edges piped in pink, matching armholes and ribbon belt threaded from side-front to tied bow at back, wide flared trousers. Blue satin slippers. **5** Cream artificial-silk dressing gown, patterned in orange, brown and yellow spots and circles, sleeveless wrapover bodice, elbow-length circular-cut cape collar, edged with orange, brown and yellow ribbons, matching side-front edge, hip-level tied bow and long ends and top of single hip-level patch pocket. Yellow satin house shoes, brown and beige feather pompon trim, high heels.

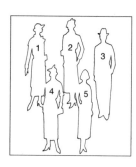

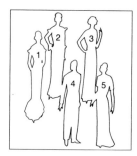

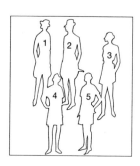

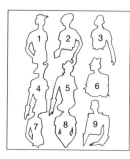

1935 Day Wear

1 Charcoal, black and pale-grey flecked wool-tweed coat-dress with horizontal rib, wrapover semi-fitted bodice, low V-shaped neckline, black suede vest infill, matching wide buttoned belt with arrow-shaped end, short shoulder cape under scarf collar tied into large bow, long inset sleeves, padded shoulders, white piqué cuffs, narrow knee-length skirt, mid-calf-length underskirt, wide box-pleat. Black straw hat, light-grey ribbon trim. Black leather clutch bag; matching shoes, bow trim, high heels.
2 Single-breasted dark-blue, grey and black wool-tweed coat, long inset sleeves, black Persian lamb 'cuffs' from wrist to above elbow and point to below padded shoulders, matching large collar, narrow skirts, hip-level piped pockets. Varnished black straw hat, asymmetric brim, self-straw trim. Black leather clutch bag and gloves. Black and white leather shoes. **3** Two-piece grey flannel suit: double-breasted jacket, wide lapels, piped pockets; wide trousers, turn-ups. Grey and white striped cotton collar-attached shirt. Red and grey striped silk tie. Grey trilby. Black leather shoes. **4** White linen two-piece suit: fitted hip-length jacket, fastening on left side with large navy-blue plastic buttons from hem to bust, square neckline, shallow collar, inset elbow-length cuffed sleeves, padded shoulders, navy-blue suede belt, asymmetric white plastic buckle; narrow panelled skirt, inverted box-pleats from knee-level. Navy-blue silk scarf with white spots; matching brimless hat. White cotton gauntlet gloves. Navy-blue leather clutch bag. Navy-blue and white leather shoes. **5** Fawn wool dress, semi-fitted bodice, padded shoulders, round neckline, bias-cut jabot fastened in four places with red plastic buttons, matching hems of raglan sleeves, belt and side-hip panel seams of flared skirt. Fawn felt hat. Beige suede shoes, red leather trim.

Evening Wear

1 White silk-organdie sleeveless evening dress spotted in black, wide neckline and combined yoke, deep gathered self-fabric frill edged with black silk ribbon and black lace, bias-cut fitted bodice and narrow skirt, wide gathered frill above ankle-length at front and mid-calf-length at back, trimmed to match yoke frill, black velvet ribbon belt knotted on right side. **2** Two-piece dark-plum velvet theatre/dinner suit: waist-length single-breasted jacket, four-button fastening, panelled semi-fitted bodice, circular black net hip yoke attached at waist under self-fabric belt, matching collar on wide neckline and cuffs of long tight inset sleeves; full-length bias-cut panelled flared skirt. Brimless pillbox hat covered with tiny black organdie flowers.
3 Bronze silk-satin formal evening dress, bias-cut bodice and full-length flared skirt cut in one piece, central seam front and back, wide extended shoulder straps draped and tied above V-shaped neckline, low back.
4 Black wool formal two-piece evening suit: double-breasted tailcoat, worn open, wide satin lapels, matching covered buttons; wide trousers, black satin ribbon trim on outside seams, no turn-ups. Double-breasted white piqué waistcoat, wide shawl collar. White starched-front shirt worn with wing collar and white bow-tie. Black patent-leather shoes. **5** Sleeveless black lace theatre/dinner dress worn over peach silk-crepe dress cut on same lines, V-shaped neckline, panelled bodice, full-length bias-cut panelled skirt, slight train. Waist-length black velvet jacket, bias-cut waterfall collar, ends tied and knotted on centre-front waist, circular-cut elbow-length sleeves, padded shoulders.

Sports and Leisure Wear

1 Riding. Hip-length moss-green, fawn and tan flecked wool-tweed fitted jacket, single-breasted fastening, panel seams, wide lapels, tight inset sleeves, button trim, diagonal welt pockets below waist. Fawn twill jodhpurs, turn-ups, stitched panel on inside leg at knee level. Fawn wool sweater. Green, tan and cream striped silk scarf worn at neck. Moss-green felt hat worn at an angle, curled brim. Brown leather gloves; matching lace-up ankle-boots.
2 Riding. Dark-green wool single-breasted jacket, three-button fastening, wide lapels, inset sleeves, stitched cuffs, button trim, patch pockets with inverted box-pleats. Light-brown twill jodhpurs, full to above knees, buttoned over knees, worn tucked into long brown leather boots. Cream wool collar-attached shirt. Pale-green, grey and tan checked wool tie. Brown trilby. Brown leather gloves.
3 Beach wear. Yellow cotton two-piece: orange and green large spot pattern, short top, halter-neck gathered onto white cotton rope, tied at front into large bow; flared shorts cut without waistband, wide legs, central crease. Yellow and white checked cotton shoes, self-fabric rouleau bow fastening, flat heels.
4 Tennis. Cream machine-knitted cotton, ribbed design, open collar, narrow shoulder yoke continued into short dolman sleeves, bodice bloused into waistband. Short white linen culottes, knife-pleats from waist to low hip-level. White cotton ankle-socks. White canvas lace-up sports shoes. **5** Beach wear. Pink, navy-blue and white checked cotton combination blouse and shorts, strap opening from hip-level to under pointed revers, large white plastic buttons, matching trim on breast patch pockets and large buckle on belt, short sleeves, padded shoulders, shorts with wide leg. Navy-blue leather shoes, strap-and-bow fastening, flat heels.

Blouses and Accessories

1 Hip-length blue linen collarless blouse, left side fastening, square neckline, large navy-blue plastic buttons, short inset sleeves, top-stitched satin binding, matching belt and patch pocket, padded shoulders. Navy-blue felt hat, split brim, top-stitched satin trim. **2** Brown and beige striped taffeta collarless blouse, round neckline, bias-cut facing, top-stitched detail, matching short inset sleeves and side panels in bodice, narrow waistband, plastic bow trim. Brown felt hat worn at an angle, cream petersham bow trim. Brown leather clutch bag; matching gloves. **3** Pale-blue silk-crepe blouse, pattern of pink flowers, scarf collar tied into large bow, short dolman sleeves, padded shoulders. Navy-blue suede belt, round buckle. **4** Hip-length dark-brown linen blouse, large cream linen collar matching cuffs of short raglan-style sleeves, centre-front zip fastening, button trim, top-stitched self-fabric detail. Beige felt hat, brown ribbon trim. Beige leather gauntlet gloves, bow trim. **5** White frilled organdie jabot, bow trim, wing collar. Navy-blue linen jacket, wide lapels. Navy-blue felt hat. Navy-blue leather gauntlet gloves. **6** Cream artificial-silk blouse, strap fastening, shirt collar, shoulder yoke, short inset sleeves, padded shoulders, small breast patch pocket. Brown lacquered-straw hat, fancy crown. **7** Hip-length cream crepe-de-chine collarless blouse, shaped seams under bust, cream crepe-de-chine raglan sleeves patterned with outsized bright-pink spots. **8** Oatmeal silk blouse, short raglan-style sleeves, pink, yellow and pale-blue checked taffeta pleated jabot. Wide pink leather belt, round buckle. Cream straw hat, pink ribbon trim. **9** Red and white spotted silk blouse, long inset sleeves trimmed from wrist to elbow with pleated white organdie, matching collar and front opening to bust-level.

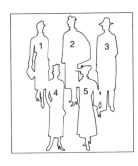

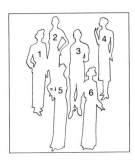

1936 Day Wear

1 Pale-blue and cream linen two-piece suit: semi-fitted top, double-breasted fastening between two small bust-level patch pockets and under narrow roll collar, long inset sleeves, padded shoulders, dark-blue linen belt fastening under bow trim; flared skirt, box-pleats sewn to low hip-level. Light-brown silk scarf worn in V-shaped neckline. Dark-blue brimless hat. Cream gauntlet gloves. Navy-blue leather clutch bag; matching shoes, stacked heels. **2** Hip-length green wool cape, front edges bound in brown leather, padded shoulders, matching flared skirt. Beige wool collarless single-breasted jacket, fastened with self-fabric covered buttons in two sets of three, single patch pocket above brown leather buckled belt and two below. Brown felt hat, asymmetric truncated crown. Beige leather gauntlets. Brown leather bar-strap shoes. **3** Fawn rainproofed wool overcoat, fly fastening under wide lapels, raglan sleeves, button trim, flap pockets. Striped wool trousers, wide legs, turn-ups. Brown felt trilby. Brown leather gloves and lace-up shoes. **4** Bottle-green wool collarless coat-dress, single-breasted fastening with large black buttons, high neckline, matching belt buckle, long cuffed sleeves, gathers from shoulder yoke/epaulettes, flared skirt, wide knife-pleats sewn to low hip. Black felt pillbox hat with green silk roses. Black clutch bag. Black and white leather shoes. **5** Pale-yellow lightweight wool coat-dress, single-breasted fastening with large buttons from tie-belt to under matching scarf collar, dropped and padded shoulderline, three-quarter-length panelled sleeves, narrow cuffs, seams of panelled bodice continued into flared skirt from waist to hem. Dark-ochre felt hat, wide brim split to form peak at front, self-trim. Cream gauntlet gloves. Brown leather shoes.

Evening Wear

1 Cream synthetic-and-wool mixture dinner jacket, single-breasted, single-button fastening, wide lapels faced with silk, flap pockets. Black mohair trousers, wide legs, silk braid trim on outside seam, no turn-ups. Black silk pleated cummerbund, matching bow-tie. White piqué collar-attached shirt. Black leather shoes. **2** Rust silk-crepe evening dress, semi-fitted bodice, low draped décolletage, self-fabric padded and twisted shoulder straps, narrow belt, clasp fastening, bustle attached to back of belt, bias-cut skirt, slight train at back. **3** Dull-mulberry crepe dinner dress, single-breasted bloused bodice, three-button fastening to under bust, hook-and-bar fastening under collar, button trim, padded shoulders, dropped sleeve head, long wide inset sleeves, wide self-fabric belt, button fastening, hip-level narrow circular skirt, curved central split to above ankles, hip-level triangular flap pockets set at an angle. Hat in matching fabric, pointed crown, twisted padded brim. Black satin shoes, crossed straps. **4** Red silk-velvet dinner/theatre dress, bloused bodice, low V-shaped neckline, deep armholes edged with wide band of stiffened gold tissue, matching set of covered buttons on either side centre-front seam, padded shoulders, draped skirt, pleated floating panel from waist to ground at front, short train at back. **5** Dull-moss-green crepe evening dress, ruched bodice, narrow shoulder straps hidden under pleated pale-grey silk chiffon, trails to ground at back, brooch trim on neck edge, panelled skirt flared from knee-level with circular-cut inset godets.

Sports and Leisure Wear

1 Country wear. Ochre, beige and tan checked wool-tweed two-piece suit: single-breasted fitted jacket, three-button fastening from waist to under wide lapels, full-length fitted inset sleeves, padded shoulders, patch-and-flap pockets; narrow skirt, centre-front split from hem to below knee. Cream crepe blouse. Tan felt hat, feather trim. Light-brown leather envelope clutch bag, matching gloves. Brown and tan leather lace-up shoes, high-stacked heels. **2** Ski wear. Two-piece bottle-green wool suit: hip-length double-breasted belted jacket, fastening from hem to under stand collar, inset sleeves, large hip-level patch-and-flap pockets; wide trousers gathered into buttoned cuffs on ankle. Cream silk scarf at neck. Knitted rust wool hat, pompon trim. Knitted cream wool gauntlet mittens. Dark-green leather lace-up boots. **3** Holiday wear. Grey and cream striped linen two-piece suit: single-breasted jacket, single-button fastening, wide lapels, flap pockets; wide trousers, turn-ups. Cream cotton collar-attached shirt. Green, tan and grey striped silk tie. Natural straw boater, green ribbon band. Tan leather gloves and lace-up shoes. **4** Country wear. Green, brown and red checked wool single-breasted overcoat, raglan sleeves, large collar, wide lapels, flap pockets. Plus-fours in matching fabric. Green and red spotted silk scarf. Brown wool-tweed peaked cap. Brown leather gloves and lace-up shoes. **5** Holiday wear. Pale yellow artificial-silk dress patterned in brown, round neckline, top-stitched facing, matching panel seams and hip-level patch pockets, short flared raglan sleeves, padded shoulders, bloused bodice, cord lacing decoration each side centre-front from neck to bustline, flared skirt, panel seams end in pleats, white leather belt. Beige straw hat. White gloves and shoes.

Underwear and Negligee

1 White artificial-silk two-piece pyjama suit: hip-length top, unfitted and gathered from shoulder yoke seam, tie-belt, buttoned strap fastening from bust-level to under peter-pan collar, long inset sleeves gathered into narrow cuffs, appliqué flowers and leaf motifs in pinks, blues and greens decorate upper part of bodice; matching wide hems of flared trousers. Pink leather moccasins. **2** Peach satin brassiere, fitted cups covered in peach lace, adjustable shoulder straps, back fastening. Cream perforated latex girdle, elasticated front gusset and waistband, four adjustable and detachable suspenders. Pale-flesh silk stockings. **3** Salmon-pink light-weight knitted-wool unit-suit: sleeveless vest with V-shaped neckline, front strap fastening, rubber buttons; knickers with short pant legs. Brown wool carpet slippers. **4** Pale-turquoise silk slip, neck edge trimmed with coffee lace matching hemline of flared skirt, shaped side panels from underarm, self-fabric rouleau shoulder straps. Turquoise velvet mules. **5** Pale-blue silk nightdress, draped neckline, armholes shaped into neck, trimmed with cream lace, shaped seam under bust, ground-length bias-cut flared skirt. **6** Salmon-pink artificial-silk negligee, high round neckline gathered in by self-colour ribbon, matching tie at waist-level, full-length bishop-style inset sleeves gathered into padded shoulders and into ruched elasticated bands at wrist-level, ground-length full skirt and bodice cut in one piece.

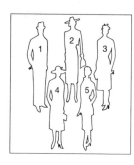

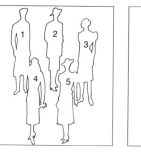

1937 Day Wear

1 Three-piece light-grey and charcoal striped wool suit: single-breasted jacket, three-button fastening, wide lapels, flap pockets; collarless single-breasted waistcoat; wide trousers with turn-ups. Fawn and white striped cotton collar-attached shirt. Grey, brown and tan striped silk tie. Grey trilby. Black leather gloves and shoes. **2** Short brown linen collarless bolero-style jacket, edge-to-edge, long inset sleeves, padded shoulders, mock-flap pockets. Cream linen dress, top-stitched, buttoned step opening from bust to under round neckline, flared skirt, inverted box-pleat from above knee-level to hemline, brown leather belt, large gilt buckle. Brown felt hat, cream silk drapery. Cream gauntlet gloves. Brown leather bag. Brown and cream leather shoes. **3** Fawn and rust checked wool collarless double-breasted coat, large buttons under high neckline and on waistline, small mock-flap pockets on bust and hip-level, long inset sleeves, padded shoulders, flared skirt. Rust silk scarf. Brown felt hat, narrow curled brim. Brown leather bag, gloves and shoes. **4** Navy-blue linen collarless coat, edge-to-edge, loop-and-button fastening on waist, fitted panelled bodice and flared skirt cut in one piece, full-length inset sleeves, padded shoulders, navy-blue suede flower. Collarless white linen dress patterned with red birds. Navy-blue lacquered-straw hat, shallow crown trimmed with white ribbon bow, wide brim. White cotton gauntlet gloves. Navy-blue leather bag. Navy-blue and white leather shoes. **5** Dark-red lightweight wool dress, bloused bodice, shaped seam under bust, ruched either side central seam, wing collar, full-length inset sleeves, padded shoulders, two-tier flared skirts, wide black suede belt knotted into bow on centre front. Black suede shoes, bow trim.

Wedding Wear

1 Cream silk-crepe two-piece: wrapover jacket, long shawl collar, draped tied belt, waterfall ends, inset sleeves, full from padded shoulders, gathered at elbow-level, tight and ruched from elbow to wrist-level, pointed hem, button fastening from wrist to elbow; full-length dress, cowl neckline, panelled flared skirt, slight train. Brimless hat, covered in cream silk, edged with pearls; short cream net veil. **2** Bias-cut oyster satin wedding dress, high round neckline edged with two rows of pearl-edged embroidered net, matching net on gathered puff oversleeves and pearl-edged hem of tight undersleeves, fitted bodice, seam from centre-front under bust to bust point to side seams above waist, fitted skirt, short train. Ground-length Edwardian lace veil, scalloped edges; heart-shaped headdress of wax flowers and pearls. **3** White silk-crepe wedding dress, draped neckline between raglan seams of white silk-chiffon sleeves, flared to wrists and below, bias-cut bodice and skirt cut in one piece, short train. White pleated silk fan-shaped headdress; long silk-tulle veil, embroidered edges. **4** Turquoise satin bridesmaid's dress, pattern of pink, white, pale-blue and pale-green flowers and leaves, padded shoulders, short inset puff sleeves gathered into narrow bands, semi-fitted bodice, centre-front seam from bust-level to under V-shaped neckline, velvet ribbon belt, round buckle, flared skirt. Turquoise straw hat, rouleau band and bow in dress fabric. **5** Pale-pink silk-taffeta wedding dress, high round neckline, small mandarin collar, padded shoulders, short puffed oversleeves, tight undersleeves ruched from wrist to elbow, decorative pearl-button trim, matching centre-front seam from under neckline to low hip-level flared skirt. Pale-pink silk-organdie headdress, pearl trim; long pink silk-tulle veil.

Sports and Leisure Wear

1 Country wear. Two-piece brown and black flecked wool-tweed suit: single-breasted jacket, three-button fastening, narrow lapels, flap pockets, knee-length plus-fours. Hand-knitted brown wool sweater. Cream collar-attached shirt. Brown wool-tweed tie. Brown wool-tweed peaked cap. Long beige wool socks. Brown and tan leather lace-up shoes. **2** Country wear. Bottle-green, cream and rust checked wool seven-eighths-length coat, single-breasted, single-button fastening, wide lapels, padded shoulders, inset sleeves, buttoned cuffs, patch pockets. Bottle-green wool skirt, centre-front knife-pleat. Cream wool scarf. Bottle-green felt hat, small crown, rust ribbon band. Brown leather shoes. **3** Tennis. White cotton dress, bloused bodice, stepped button fastening under round neckline, vertical epaulettes, padded shoulders, puff sleeves, wide self-fabric buckled belt, flared skirt, small hip-level patch pockets set at an angle, facing knife-pleats from pocket points. White cotton ankle-socks. White sports shoes. **4** Country wear. Double-breasted tan wool coat, wide lapels, outsized collar, padded shoulders, long sleeves, button trim, self-fabric buckled belt, hip-level patch-and-flap pockets, flared skirts. Cream and green patterned silk scarf. Brown felt hat, shallow rounded crown, self-felt trim. Brown leather gloves and shoes. **5** Holiday wear. Pale-blue artificial-silk two-piece suit patterned in white and fawn circles: short fitted single-breasted jacket, three self-fabric-covered buttons under wide lapels, padded shoulders, puff sleeves, waist-level mock-flap pockets; flared skirt, pintucked panels from hip yoke. Beige lacquered-straw hat, small crown, flat top, wide brim, yellow and white felt flower trim. White gloves. Light-brown leather bag and shoes.

Footwear

1 Brown suede shoes, high vamps, open sides, leather heels. **2** Dark-green leather lace-up shoes, no toecaps, decorative top-stitching. **3** Cream leather shoes, donkey-brown leather trim on toes, matching high heels. **4** Navy-blue leather shoes, high vamps, button-and-strap trim, high heels. **5** Black satin dance shoes, red linings, wide bar straps, covered button fastening, high heels. **6** White kid shoes, navy-blue trim, matching high heels. **7** Cream leather lace-up brogues, brown toecaps and trim, perforated detail. **8** Wine suede shoes, self-suede looped trim, high heels. **9** White canvas shoes, navy-blue leather toecaps and trim, matching high heels. **10** Black leather shoes, high strap-and-buckle fastening. **11** Tan leather sandals, open sides, matching detail on front, strap-and-buckle fastening. **12** Donkey-brown leather shoes, high vamps, ribbon lace-up fastening, high heels. **13** Black suede evening shoes, gold kid linings, black satin bar straps, high slender heels. **14** Bottle-green calf-leather shoes, high tongues, self-leather buckles, high heels. **15** Black leather lace-up shoes, top-stitched trim. **16** Silver kid evening sandals, open sides, matching details on front, ankle straps, high slender heels. **17** Navy-blue leather shoes, wide white leather inserted trim, high heels. **18** Brown lace-up country brogues, perforated detail. **19** Cream kid shoes, black patent-leather toecaps and high heels. **20** Black leather shoes, stitched detail, high heels. **21** Brown suede shoes, tan leather shaped toecaps, high heels. **22** Olive-green leather shoes, self-leather roll trim, high slender heels. **23** Black leather shoes, stitched detail, high heels. **24** Ginger-brown leather shoes, high tongues, self-leather covered buckles, high stacked heels.

1938 Day Wear

1 Lightweight navy-blue wool dress, high round neckline trimmed with white cotton piqué tabs, navy-blue and white spotted silk scarf set into diagonal panel seams, long inset sleeves, padded shoulders, self-fabric belt, plastic buckle, flared skirt, seamed side panels, end front-facing knife pleats. Navy-blue suede shoes, chain trim.

2 Navy-blue wool two-piece suit: double-breasted fitted jacket, two-button fastening under wide lapels, flap pockets; straight-cut trousers, turn-ups. White collar-attached shirt. Striped silk tie. Navy-blue trilby, black ribbon band. Black leather shoes.

3 Pale-green linen mixture two-piece suit: edge-to-edge collarless cardigan jacket, long sleeves, padded shoulders, hip-level patch pockets, self-fabric buckled belt; straight skirt, wide front panel. Brown silk blouse, bow-tie neckline. White straw hat, small crown, asymmetric brim, brown ribbon trim. White gloves. Brown leather handbag; matching leather shoes, diagonal bar straps, high heels.

4 Pale-blue washable-silk dress, button fastening from hem to under tiny collar, top-stitched panel seams from padded shoulders to above knee-level end in inverted box-pleats, top-stitching repeated on hems of puff sleeves, on narrow belt, on hip-level pockets and on covered buttons. Brown lacquered-straw hat, tiny flat-topped crown, white ribbon trim, wide stiff brim. Large brown leather handbag, matching shoes, high tongues, openwork, high heels.

5 Dark-beige wool single-breasted coat, two-button fastening, hip-length shaped front panel in leopard-patterned cloth, incorporating pockets, large collar, padded shoulders, long inset sleeves, flared skirts. Tan felt hat, flat circular brim, upturned edge, small crown, narrow self-fabric strap at back. Cream leather shoes, tan leather toecaps and bow trim.

Evening Wear

1 Evening coat in multicoloured brocade on gold background, single-breasted fastening with small gilt flower-shaped buttons from above knee-level to under outsized lapels, fitted bodice, padded shoulders, short puff sleeves, ground-length flared panelled skirts. Long white kid gloves. Small gold sequined bag. Gold kid strap sandals. 2 Deep-wine taffeta evening dress, fitted bodice shirred on centre-front seam from curved hip seam to low neckline, wide shoulder straps, self-fabric ground-length underskirt gathered from hip, spotted net overskirt, frilled self-fabric trim at knee-level and on hem. 3 Two-piece dinner ensemble: hip-length oyster silk-satin blouse, collar and rever-shaped seams from padded shoulders to side hem, V-shaped neckline faced to below bust, tassel trim, horizontal pintucked yoke matching upper part of short puff sleeves, side-hip panels from waist to hem and half-belt with vertical pintucks; ground-length black velvet skirt. 4 Multicoloured printed silk-crepe dinner dress on black background, fitted bodice, curved seams from side waist to under square keyhole below high round neckline, padded shoulders, short puff sleeves, wide self-fabric tie-belt, ground-length flared skirt. Elbow-length black silk gloves. 5 Two-piece black wool evening suit: single-breasted fitted jacket, linked-button fastening under wide lapels, bound pockets; straight-cut trousers, braid trim on outside seams, no turn-ups. White cotton piqué shirt worn with wing collar. Black satin bow-tie. Black patent-leather shoes.

Sports and Leisure Wear

1 Beach wear. Ankle-length pale-green towelling beach coat, multicoloured outsized flower print, single-breasted fastening from mid-calf level to under long pointed green satin top-stitched collar which matches cuffs of elbow-length puffed sleeves, buttoned belt and covered buttons; fitted bodice, padded shoulders, hip-level pockets in side seams of flared skirts. Green leather strap sandals, peep-toes, platform soles. 2 Skating. Dark-green machine-knitted sweater, ribbed polo collar matching cuffs of long inset sleeves, padded shoulders. Thigh-length navy-blue wool gored skirt, narrow waistband, button fastening. Long navy-blue leather boots. 3 Holiday wear. Three-piece cruising suit in heavyweight navy-blue silk: collarless edge-to-edge thigh-length jacket, long flared sleeves, padded shoulders, hip-level patch pockets trimmed with natural and sandstone silk; matching single-breasted blouse, fastening from waist to under pointed collar; ankle-length wide flared trousers, central creases and turn-ups, waistband decorated with three buttons. Navy-blue canvas sandals, peep-toes, wooden platform soles and short thick heels. 4 Tennis. Single-breasted collarless white linen blouse, short inset sleeves, curved half-yoke from under arm to mid-shoulder, small breast pockets, decorative blue silk handkerchief in left pocket. Tailored white linen flared shorts, central top-stitched seams end in inverted box-pleats, top-stitched belt and buckle. White ankle-socks and sports shoes. 5 Tennis. White machine-knitted cotton shirt, pointed collar, short buttoned-strap opening, short sleeves. Tailored white linen shorts, zipped fly, buttoned waistband, pleats and central creases, slanted side pockets, no turn-ups. White ankle-socks and sports shoes.

Underwear and Negligee

1 Two-piece pale-blue washable-satin pyjama suit: fitted top trimmed with three diagonal pink satin ribbons on each side from side seams to under pleated peter-pan collar, matching trim on elbow-length puffed sleeves and bow trim over keyhole opening; ground-length flared trousers, fitted over hips, narrow waistband. Pale-blue peep-toe slippers. 2 Green spotted cream silk dressing gown, wrapover front, bloused bodice, padded shoulders, full-length bishop-style sleeves, deep cuffs, skirts fitted over hips to ground-length, hip-level patch pockets, outsized revers faced with white spotted green silk, matching lining of wide tie-belt. 3 Vest and knicker set in machine-knitted peach silk: hip-length vest top, lace-edged neckline, narrow satin ribbon shoulder straps, deep rib from under bust to hip, elasticated waist rib; long fitted knickers, wide rib at hem, elasticated waistband. Peach velvet mules, high heels. 4 Pale-green washable-silk nightdress, bloused bodice pintucked under arms and across front bustline, edged at neck with self-fabric ruched frills, matching pintucked shoulder straps, narrow self-fabric tie-belt, ground-length flared skirt. 5 Black satin cami-knickers, trimmed on neck edge and diagonally over bust with inset flat rouleau embroidery, matching shoulder straps, fitted bodice, shaped seam under bust, knickers fitted over hips, wide flare to hem, fine lace edging. Black velvet mules, black satin rosettes and trim, high heels.

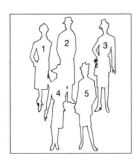

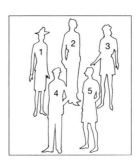

1939 Day Wear

1 Edge-to-edge light-brown wool-tweed coat, held at waist by buckled self-fabric belt and at bust-level with a hook and bar, narrow fur collar matching cuffs of long inset sleeves, trim on shaped yoke seam and hip-level seams incorporating pockets, flared skirts. Wine felt hat, self-colour ribbon trim. Brown leather handbag and gloves; matching shoes. **2** Single-breasted fawn, grey and tan checked wool-tweed overcoat, three-button fastening under wide lapels, cuffed raglan sleeves, vertical hip-level welt pockets, top-stitched edges and detail. Grey wool trousers. Tan wool scarf. Collar-attached shirt. Tweed tie. Grey felt trilby. Brown leather gloves and shoes. **3** Two-piece rust, cream and fawn flecked wool-tweed suit: hip-length edge-to-edge jacket, held at waist by wide rust leather tie-belt and with hook and bar under leopard-skin collar, matching panels under bust to hemline, cut away over side hips, padded shoulders, long inset sleeves; flared skirt. Brimless fawn felt hat, rust silk trim. Black leather handbag and gloves, matching sling-back shoes, peep-toes, high heels. **4** Silk dress, slightly bloused collarless bodice, patterned blue, lilac and pink on navy-blue background, gathers between half-yoke seams above bust and shaped seam above waist, elbow-length puff sleeves, plain navy-blue silk flared panelled skirt, self-fabric belt. Blue straw hat, pink ribbon trim. Pink gloves. Navy-blue leather shoes, cross straps, peep-toes. **5** Hip-length fawn wool unfitted jacket, single-breasted fastening from bust-level to under stand collar, curved half-shoulder yoke joined to vertical side-panel seams, hip-level welt pockets, long cuffed sleeves. Light-brown wool skirt. Fawn felt hat, navy-blue ribbon trim. Fawn leather gloves. Fawn and navy-blue leather shoes, perforated decoration.

Evening Wear

1 Pearl-grey evening dress, finely pleated fitted bodice, low neckline, narrow self-fabric rouleau shoulder straps, deep waist inset of pearl-grey satin, ground-length sunray-pleated skirt; dress worn over a slip of primrose-yellow silk. Grey satin muff decorated with Iceland poppies in tea-rose-pink and soft-orange. **2** Royal-blue silk-crepe evening dress, strapless boned bodice shirred in three vertical lines, three-tier skirt, knee-length top skirt, longer at back, draped from side hip to side hip, mid-calf-length middle tier, longer at back, ground-length third tier. Royal-blue satin strap sandals, peep-toes, thin platform soles. **3** White silk-chiffon evening dress, hand-painted design of large garlands of anemones in tones of pink, mauve, pale-blue and apple-green, high waist seam under bust, wide self-fabric shoulder straps, fitted panelled bodice and ground-length flared skirt cut in one piece with no waist seam. Long apple-green silk gloves. **4** Dinner ensemble: collarless fitted jacket, wide horizontal stripes of black, red, silver and gold sequins, edge of V-shaped neckline and front edges bound in black satin, gold and black glass buttons, long tight sleeves, pleated heads, padded shoulders. Ground-length black velvet flared skirt. Black satin shoes, peep-toes. **5** Cream rayon-organdie evening dress patterned with pale-sea-green fern leaves, hip-length fitted bodice, sweetheart neckline, short puff sleeves, worn over strapless boned underbodice in plain cream rayon, matching ground-length skirts, each gathered into scalloped hip seam. Pink and pale-green silk flower hair decoration. Pale-sea-green purse.

Sports and Leisure Wear

1 Golf. Two-piece brown, fawn and green checked wool-tweed suit: fitted edge-to-edge jacket, linked-button fastening under notched shawl collar in plain brown wool-tweed, matching stitched cuffs of long inset sleeves, hip-level flap pockets and side panels of skirt, front panel wide box-pleat. Collarless single-breasted flannel waistcoat. Cream silk scarf in neck. Fawn felt hat, truncated crown, wide brim. Brown and cream leather lace-up shoes. **2** Winter sports. Two-piece wine-red waterproofed wool-gaberdine suit: single-breasted jacket fastening from hip-level to under wide lapels, six welt pockets with button trim, black patent-leather buckled belt, long inset sleeves; full trousers gathered into cuffs at ankle level. Black knitted-wool scarf and pixie hood. Lambswool gauntlet mittens. Black boots. **3** Boating. Yellow linen blouse, button fastening from waist to under open collar, short sleeves, stitched cuffs, yoke seam above bust, two inset mock-pointed flap pockets. Navy-blue linen flared shorts, side-hip pockets, button trim, matching waistband. White ankle-socks. Lace-up navy-blue canvas shoes with rope soles. **4** Golf. Single-breasted brown and beige flecked wool-tweed jacket, three-button fastening, wide lapels, large patch pockets. Light-brown flannel trousers, straight-cut legs, turn-ups. Green knitted-wool sweater, V-shaped neckline. Cream cotton shirt. Rust wool tie. Light-brown wool-tweed peaked cap. Brown and beige leather shoes. **5** Boating. Blue, white and green striped cotton shirt, pointed collar worn open, short sleeves, stitched cuffs, large chest-level patch pockets with buttoned flaps. Navy-blue linen shorts, wide legs, no turn-ups. Navy-blue canvas step-in shoes, rope soles.

Accessories

1 Beige felt beret, top-stitched detail. Brown velvet scarf. **2** Grey felt hat, pleated brim, fur trim. **3** Navy-blue leather shoes, high vamps, ribbon laces, top-stitched detail, high heels. **4** Brimless black felt hat, top-stitched edges and detail, pink and grey pleated organdie fans at back. **5** Green felt hat, tall crown, gold satin ribbon trim. **6** Bottle-green and white leather shoes, top-stitched detail, ribbon laces, high heels. **7** Black and white leather shoes, ribbon laces. **8** Wine-red suede shoes, wide bar straps, black pleated-leather bow trim, medium heels. **9** Cream linen hat, top-stitched asymmetric crown, wide brim. **10** Small grey felt hat, tiny crown, upswept narrow brim, green feather trim. **11** Navy-blue and grey bar-strap shoes, ribbon laces, high heels. **12** Blue felt hat, pleated crown, self-felt bow trim. **13** Deep-purple felt hat, shallow crown, flat top, upswept brim, fine veil. **14** Mustard-yellow felt hat, wide upswept brim, black petersham ribbon trim. Fur scarf. **15** Brown leather shoes, pleated fan-shaped tongues, high heels. **16** Natural leather strap sandals, leather thong fastening, low wooden heels and platform soles. **17** Brown leather bag, ruched detail, rouleau handles and trim. **18** Dark-green leather bag, long handle, zip fastening. **19** Navy-blue leather bag, metal frame, rouleau handles, zip fastening. **20** Pale-pink straw hat, wide brim, shallow crown, pink and white petersham ribbon trim. **21** Cream leather sling-back shoes, peep-toes, top-stitched detail, high heels, platform soles. **22** Brown leather bag, metal frame, short handle, gilt monogram. **23** Apple-green leather strap sandals, open sides, peep-toes, low thick heels. **24** Grey leather shoes, elasticated sides, perforated detail, medium heels. **25** Tiny brown straw top hat, ribbon trim. **26** Leather sandals, peep-toes, wooden platform soles.

Chart of the Development of 1930s Fashion
Biographies of Designers
Sources for 1930s Fashion

Chart of the Development of 1930s Fashion

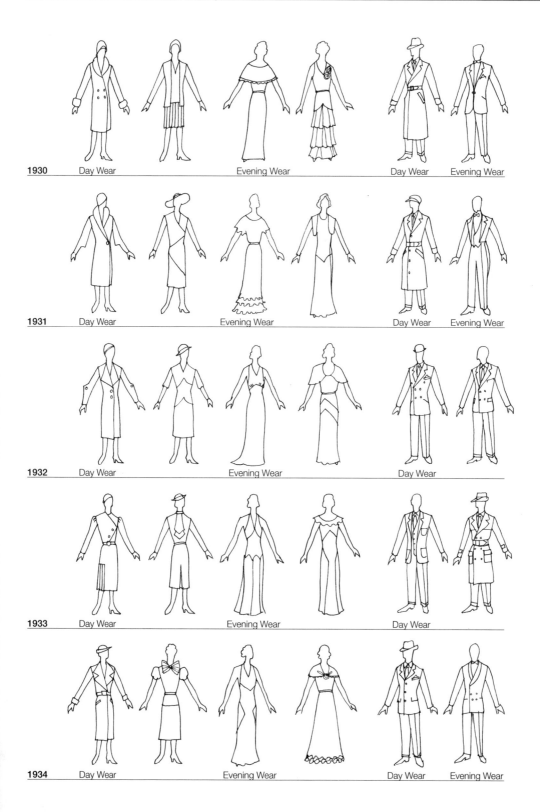

1930 Day Wear Evening Wear Day Wear Evening Wear

1931 Day Wear Evening Wear Day Wear Evening Wear

1932 Day Wear Evening Wear Day Wear

1933 Day Wear Evening Wear Day Wear

1934 Day Wear Evening Wear Day Wear Evening Wear

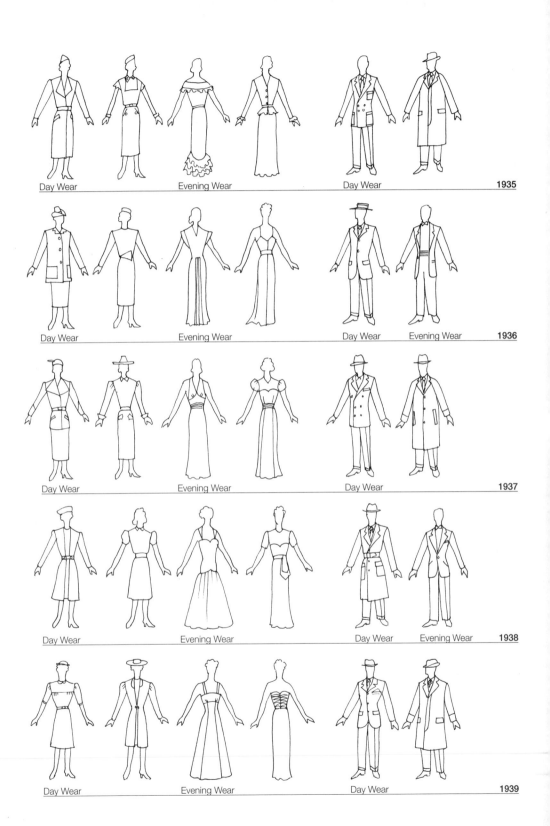

Day Wear   Evening Wear   Day Wear   **1935**

Day Wear   Evening Wear   Day Wear   Evening Wear   **1936**

Day Wear   Evening Wear   Day Wear   **1937**

Day Wear   Evening Wear   Day Wear   Evening Wear   **1938**

Day Wear   Evening Wear   Day Wear   **1939**

Biographies of Designers

Adrian (Adrian Adolph Greenburg) 1903–59. Costume designer. Born Naugatuck, Connecticut, USA. In the 1930s Adrian was Hollywood's most influential designer. His many widely copied designs include a slouch hat worn by Greta Garbo in the 1929 film *A Woman of Affairs* and a white organdie dress with ruffled sleeves created for Joan Crawford in *Letty Lynton* in 1932. As well as his work for films, he also made chic, wearable suits, sometimes decorated with appliqué. He retired as a costume designer in 1942.

Augustabernard (Augusta Bernard) 1886–1946. Designer. Born Biarritz, France. Augustabernard opened her own business in Biarritz in 1920, moving to Paris in 1923. She became famous for dramatic, well-cut evening dresses in pale, sombre colours and for uncomplicated day clothes, often in tweed. She was known for decorating her elegant, slender evening gowns with flounces, scalloped tiers and scarves attached at the hip or shoulder. She retired in 1934.

Bruyère, Marie-Louise Dates unknown. Designer. Bruyère trained at Callot Soeurs, joined Lanvin in 1920 and opened her own house in 1928. She had a reputation for exclusivity. In the 1930s, her three-quarter-length coats worn over afternoon dresses were particularly successful.

Carnegie, Hattie (Henrietta Kanengeiser) 1889–1956. Designer, manufacturer. Born Vienna, Austria. Carnegie began her career at the age of 15 at Macy's department store, New York, dressing hats. She moved into clothing design in 1913 and launched her first collection in 1918. Her first ready-to-wear collection followed in 1928. Carnegie was best known for grey tailored suits and black dresses which she sold in her own retail stores across America. Her success was largely due to an ability to adapt Paris haute-couture fashions to the US market, where her smart but conventional clothes became highly sought after.

Chanel, Gabrielle (Coco) 1883–1971. Born Saumur, France. Chanel began her career as a milliner in Paris in 1910,

under the label 'Chanel Mode'. In 1913 she opened her first hat shop in Deauville and two years later started a dress shop in Biarritz. In 1916 she introduced jersey, and her first published design, for a chemise dress, appeared in *Harper's Bazaar*. The 1920s saw her career flourish with the founding of her Paris house and the launch of her most famous perfume, 'No. 5'. In the same decade she was responsible for introducing the 'little black dress', wide-legged yatching pants, lightweight evening chemises, geometrically patterned beaded dresses and the first of her famous tweed suits. She also began her unconventional mixing of fabrics – plain with patterned jersey, or tweed with floral silk. In the 1930s Chanel continued to develop her range of costume jewelry; her long gilt chains, rows of pearls and mixtures of semi-precious stones achieved particular popularity. During this period her evening wear became more feminine and ornate, though she also began using fabrics such as linen and cotton organdie which had previously been used only for day clothes. Chanel closed her house in 1939 but reopened in 1954, with the launch of a jersey suit, the 'No. 5'. Among the other styles associated with her name are braid-trimmed collarless cardigan-jackets, slingback two-tone sandals and handbags with gilt chains.

Daché, Lilly 1904–89. Milliner. Born Bègles, France. After an apprenticeship with a milliner in Bordeaux, Daché worked briefly for Suzanne Talbot and then for Caroline Reboux in Paris. In 1924 she joined a small New York milliners, which she bought out almost immediately. She quickly became famous for her turbans, cloche hats, snoods and caps.

Grès Couture house. Founded in 1941 by Paris-born Germaine Krebs (1903-93). Krebs trained with Premet and in 1934 she opened a couture house, 'Alix', in association with Julie Barton. 'Alix' closed in 1939. 'Madame Grès', as Krebs became known at her own house, was famous for draped and pleated dresses – in silk and wool – which resemble classical Greek robes, often cut on the bias and with dolman sleeves. She adopted a sculptural approach to dressmaking, each

garment being modelled on the mannequin by hand with minimal use of patterns or cutting.

Hartnell, (Sir) Norman 1901–79. Designer. Born London, England. Hartnell worked at Madame Désirée, Esther's and with Lucile before opening his own premises in London in 1923. His career took off during the late 1920s when he became famous for his extravagant wedding dresses, though he also designed for the theatre and for films. He was appointed dressmaker to the British Royal Family in 1938 and created Elizabeth II's wedding dress and coronation gown as well as designing many outfits for her overseas tours. His designs were central in forming the image of the royal family. In the 1940s Hartnell went on to produce his own ready-to-wear lines.

James, Charles 1906–78. Designer. Born Sandhurst, England. James began his fashion career when he opened a hat shop in Chicago in 1924 under the name of a schoolfriend, 'Charles Boucheron'. He created his first dress collection in New York in 1928, his first London collection in 1929, and his first Paris collection in 1934. By 1940 he had returned to New York and established a house under his own name. An architect of dress, James created superbly cut, sculpted ball gowns using large quantities of lavish fabrics often arranged asymmetrically in bunches and folds. He was also known for his highly structured coats, his dresses with spiral zips and his quilted ivory-satin jackets.

Lanvin, Jeanne 1867–1946. Designer. Born Brittany, France. After an apprenticeship with Suzanne Talbot, Lanvin opened her own millinery shop in Paris in 1890. She began making clothes commercially after customers commented on the garments she made for her younger sister and daughter. Lanvin became famous for her mother/daughter outfits which were significant in the development of fashion for blurring the distinction between clothing for different age groups. She created the basic shape for the 1920s at the beginning of World War I with the chemise dress. Other designs which became characteristic of the period include her breton suits and beaded evening dresses.

She was also the first couturier to design clothes for entire families, presenting a line of menswear in 1926. The following year the first of Lanvin's famous perfumes, 'Arpège', was produced. During the 1930s she often used parallel stitching and embroidered sequins and continued to show her famous 'robes de style' which were inspired by eighteenth-century dresses. Preferring embroidery and appliquéd motifs to patterned material, she transformed motifs from orientalism, botanical etchings and Renaissance, Aztec and modern art into her own individual designs. She also became famous for her use of a particular shade of blue which was known as 'Lanvin blue'.

Lelong, Lucien 1889–1958. Designer. Born Paris, France. Lelong trained at the Hautes Etudes des Commerciales, Paris, and established his own business after World War I. He became known for his skilful use of beautiful fabrics in creating elegant, understated dresses and evening wear. He was one of the first designers to produce stockings and lingerie. In the late 1930s Lelong designed tight-waisted, full skirts which were precursors to Dior's 'New Look' of 1947.

Louiseboulanger (Louise Boulanger) 1900–? Designer. Born France. At the age of 13 Louiseboulanger was apprenticed to a dressmaking business. She was then employed by Chéruit until she founded her own business in 1923. She created refined, graceful garments, often using heavy fabrics such as taffeta and moire in warm colours. Her innovations include the 'pouf' silhouette and knee-length evening skirts which fell to the ankles at the back. The house closed in 1939.

Mainbocher (Main Rousseau Bocher) 1891–1976. Designer. Born Chicago, USA. Mainbocher was the first American couturier to achieve success in Paris, opening his own house there in 1930. During the 1930s he became famous for embroidered, apron-style evening dresses, for his use of the bias cut and for creating a trend for 'Wallis blue' with the wedding dress he designed for the Duchess of Windsor. He opened a salon in New York in 1940.

Maxwell, Vera (Vera Huppé)
1901–. Designer. Born New York, USA. Maxwell started her career by making clothes for herself. By 1936 she was attracting the attention of the fashion press and from the late 1930s her designs were being bought by Seventh Avenue firms such as Adler and Adler. Maxwell established her own business in 1947, creating classic, wearable separates and suits, wraparound jersey dresses and riding jackets. She was influenced by men's country clothes and used natural dyes to produce autumnal tones.

McCardell, Claire 1905–58. Designer. Born Frederick, USA. During the late 1920s and 1930s McCardell worked with Richard Turk at Townley Frocks, and then for Hattie Carnegie. One of her first highly successful designs was the waistless, bias-cut 'monastic dress' of 1938. Returning to Townley Frocks in 1940 to design under her own name, McCardell produced easy-fitting clothes made from cotton, denim, gingham and jersey which were hugely influential.

Molyneux, (Captain) Edward
1891–1974. Designer. Born London, England. Molyneux began his career producing illustrations for magazines and advertisements and in 1911 was employed as a sketcher by Lucile. He opened his own couture house in Paris in 1919, becoming famous for simple tailored suits and skirts in muted tones which were seen as archetypally English in their restrained elegance. In the 1930s, a decade dominated by Schiaparelli's eccentric, humorous style, Molyneux's streamlined designs were particularly sought after. Between 1925 and 1932 he opened further branches in Monte Carlo, Cannes, Biarritz and London. Molyneux retired in 1950. An attempted comeback in 1965 was unsuccessful.

Morton, Digby 1906–83. Designer. Born Dublin, Ireland. Morton worked for Lachasse in London in the late 1920s and established his own business in 1933, becoming well known for his use of Aran knits and Donegal tweeds, often combined with silk blouses. Morton is also widely credited with having adapted the traditional tailor-made suit to make it more graceful and up-to-date.

Patou, Jean 1880–1936. Designer. Born Normandy, France. Patou opened the small firm Maison Parry in 1912, achieving a brief success before the advent of World War I forced the firm's closure. In 1919 he reopened under his own name, producing bell-skirted, high-waisted dresses. His Cubistic sweaters were also very popular. Patou was enormously influential with his sports and bathing wear which included the calf-length pleated skirts and sleeveless cardigans worn by the tennis player Suzanne Lenglen. In 1924 he initiated a trend by putting his own initials on his clothing and in 1927 was one of the first designers to revert to the natural waistline, heralding the shape which came to predominate during the 1930s. The House of Patou continued to be hugely successful after his death.

Philippe et Gaston (Philippe Hecht and Gaston Kaufmann) Couture house. After training at Jenny, Kaufmann joined Hecht to form a couture house which opened in 1922. Philippe et Gaston had particular success with their pearl-embroidered evening dresses and ensembles for day wear, continuing to attract the attention of the fashion press until the house closed in 1937.

Piguet, Robert 1901–53. Designer. Born Yverdon, Switzerland. After training as a banker, Piguet moved to Paris in 1918 and worked for Redfern and Poiret. Opening in 1933, the House of Piguet was known for romantic evening gowns and elegant suits and dresses, often in grey, beige or blue. Piguet also made costumes for the stage and frequently employed other designers, including Balmain, Dior, Galanos and Givenchy.

Ricci, Nina (Maria Nielli)
1883–1970. Designer. Born Turin, Italy. After training with a couturier, Ricci opened her own house in 1932. She worked by draping fabric round the mannequin to create distinctive, luxurious garments. Ricci designed clothes that were classical rather than innovative in style and which were popular with older clients.

Rochas, Marcel 1902–55. Designer. Born Paris, France. Rochas established his house in 1924, becoming one of the most important and influential designers of the 1930s. Inspired by Javanese and Balinese traditional costumes, he introduced broad-shouldered garments to his collections in 1933, creating a look usually attributed to Schiaparelli. Other innovative designs included sculpted wool coats with widely stitched seams, trouser suits in grey flannel and the 'guêpière' bustier of 1943. Rochas was also famous for imaginative embroidery and appliqués and bizarre decorative features such as stuffed birds and buttons shaped like butterflies, lipstick and pipes. He often worked with flower-patterned fabric and was one of the first designers to add pockets to his skirts.

Rouff, Maggy (Maggie Besançon de Wagner)
1896–1971. Designer. Born Paris, France. After working in her parent's company, Drécoll, Rouff founded her own house in 1929. She became famous for comfortable couture garments which often featured feminine details such as fichu collars, puffed sleeves, 'bustle'-draped skirts and bow motifs. During the 1930s Rouff created closely fitted dresses with shirring, sometimes decorated with diagonal tiers of ruffles. She also introduced many innovations into sportswear, including her jersey 'plus-fours'. Rouff was known for her imaginative use of colour.

Schiaparelli, Elsa 1890–1973. Designer. Born Rome, Italy. Schiaparelli moved to Paris in 1922 and opened a boutique, 'Pour le Sport', in 1927. The following year she showed her first collection. Her clothes were chic and eccentric, strongly influenced by modern art movements. She commissioned artists such as Salvador Dali and Jean Cocteau to design fabrics and accessories and produced a range of surreal garments, often with *trompe-l'oeil* effects. Her many innovations included unusually shaped buttons, padlock fastenings, lip-shaped pockets, and hats in the form of ice-cream cones, shoes or lamb cutlets. In 1933 her broad-shouldered pagoda sleeve set the basic shape for fashion until the New Look. Known for her gifted use of colour, Schiaparelli promoted 'Shocking Pink' and was the first designer to use plastic zippers decoratively.

Stiebel, Victor 1907–76. Designer. Born Durban, South Africa. Stiebel began an apprenticeship with Reville and Rossiter in 1929 and in 1932 opened his own house. He created romantic evening wear in the neo-classical style and was well known for his restrained day clothes, usually in soft fabrics such as jersey.

Valentina (Valentina Nicholaevna Sanina)
1899–1989. Designer. Born Kiev, Russia. Valentina established her house in 1928. While her daywear was often simple and practical, sometimes displaying peasant influences, she was best known for her dramatic evening wear and swirling capes. She was also a skilled designer of millinery, especially snoods, turbans and veils.

Vionnet, Madeleine
1876–1975. Born Aubervilliers, France. At the age of 11 Vionnet was apprenticed to a dressmaker. Six years later she joined the House of Vincent in Paris, rising to head seamstress after two years. In 1898 she travelled to London, where she worked for the dressmaker Kate O'Reilly. Returning to Paris in 1900, she spent two years as head seamstress at Callot Soeurs before moving to Doucet in 1907. In 1912 she opened her own house. The late 1920s and 1930s saw Vionnet at the height of her success. Always an innovative designer, she drew inspiration from many sources, in particular Ancient Greek civilization – she was much influenced by the design of the peplos. Simplicity and austerity are at the core of her work. Vionnet was a supreme technician, draping her toiles on a wooden doll to achieve perfect proportions between body and dress. She is best remembered for her mastery of the bias cut. She retired in 1939.

Worth 1858–1954. Couture house. Founded by the English couturier Charles Frederick Worth, the House of Worth remained in family hands after his death in 1895. In the 1930s the house was run first by Jean-Charles Worth, grandson of the founder, and then from 1936 by Roger and Maurice Worth, who maintained its reputation for refined, sumptuous, highly fashionable clothes. The company was eventually taken over by Paquin in 1954.

Sources for 1930s Fashion

Anderson Black, J.,
and Madge Garland
A History of Fashion, 1975.

Arnold, Janet
Patterns of Fashion 2: English Women's Dresses and Their Construction c. 1860–1940, 1966.

Baynes, Ken,
and Kate Baynes, eds.
The Shoe Show: British Shoes since 1790, 1979.

Boucher, François
A History of Costume in the West, 1965.

Bradfield, Nancy
Historical Costumes of England, 1958.
Costume in Detail, 1968.

Brooke, Iris
A History of English Costume, 1937.

Byrde, Penelope
The Male Image: Men's Fashion in Britain 1300–1970, 1979.

Carter, Ernestine
The Changing World of Fashion: 1900 to the Present, 1977.

Contini, Mila
Fashion, 1965.

Cunnington, C. Willet,
and Phillis Cunnington
The History of Underclothes, 1951.
English Women's Clothing in the Present Century, 1953.

De Courtais, Georgine
Women's Headdresses and Hairstyles, 1973.

Dorner, Jane
Fashion in the Twenties and Thirties, 1973.

Etherington-Smith, Meredith
Patou, 1983.

Ewing, Elizabeth
Fur in Dress, 1981.
Dress and Undress: A History of Women's Underwear, 1978.

Gallery of English Costume Weddings, 1976.

Ginsburg, Madeleine
Wedding Dress 1740–1970, 1981.
The Hat: Trends and Traditions, 1990.

Hall-Duncan, Nancy
The History of Fashion Photography, 1979.

Hansen, Henny Harald
Costume Cavalcade, 1956.

Harrison, Michael
The History of the Hat, 1960.

Howell, Georgina
In Vogue: Six Decades of Fashion, 1975.

Jarvis, Anthea
Brides, Wedding Clothes and Customs 1850–1980, 1983.

Kelsall, Freda
How We Used to Live: 1936–1953, 1981.

La Vine, W. Robert
In a Glamorous Fashion, 1987.

Langley-Moore, Doris
Fashion through Fashion Plates, 1971.

Laver, James
Costume, 1963.
A Concise History of Costume, 1969, revised edition 1995.

Lee-Potter, Charlie
Sportswear in Vogue, 1984.

Lynham, Ruth, ed.
Paris Fashion: The Great Designers and Their Creations, 1972.

Martin, Richard,
and Harold Koda
Jocks and Nerds: Men's Style in the Twentieth Century, 1989.
All-American: A Sportswear Tradition, 1985.

Mulvagh, Jane
Vogue: History of 20th Century Fashion, 1988.

Peacock, John
Fashion Sketchbook 1920–1960, 1977.
Costume 1066 to the 1990s, 1994.
The Chronicle of Western Costume, 1991.
20th Century Fashion, 1993.
Men's Fashion, 1996.

Robinson, Julian
The Fine Art of Fashion: An Illustrated History, 1989.
Fashion in the Thirties, 1978.

Saint Laurent, Cecil
The History of Ladies' Underwear, 1968.

Spellor, Reggie
'Scoop', What a Picture!: Photographs of the Thirties and Forties, 1981.

Viera, Mark A.
Hollywood Portraits: Classic Scene Stills 1929–1941, 1988.

Wilcox, R. Turner
The Mode in Costume, 1942.

Five Centuries of American Costume, 1963.
The Dictionary of Costume, 1969.

Yarwood, Doreen
English Costume: From the Second Century to 1967, 1952.

Magazines

Good Housekeeping, 1933, 1934.
Leach-Way Fashions, 1931–33.
Modern Weekly, 1931.
Sartorial Gazette: The Tailors' Magazine, 1930.
To-Day: The New National Weekly, 1938–1939.
Vogue, 1933–1937.
Weldon's Ladies Journal, 1934–1937.
Woman's Own, 1936–38.
Woman's Pictorial, 1939.
Woman's Weekly, 1930–1934.
Woman's World, 1937.

Practical Dressmaking and Knitting Journals

Bestway: Men's Knitted Wear, 1936, 1938.
Bestway Patterns and Transfers, 1933–1934.
Fashions for All, 1933.
Home Fashions and Home Fashions Pattern Service 1930–1934.
Leach's Home Dressmaker, 1935.
Paton's and Baldwin's Knitting Books, 1930, 1935.
Roma's Pattern Book, 1937.
Simplicity Pattern Book, 1938.
Vogue Pattern Book, 1937, 1938, 1939.

Trade Journals, Catalogues, etc.

Bradley's Catalogue, Summer 1938.
Bradley's Catalogue: Sale, Winter 1939.
Furs of Distinction, 1934–1935.
Laver, James
Beau Brummell Was Right, Catalogue published by Moss Bros, 1960s.
Lilley and Skinner: Shoe Catalogue, 1935–1936.
Pall Mall: Fashions for Ladies, Spring 1938, Autumn 1938, Winter 1939.
Perfection in Style and Quality Gentleman's Wear, 1934–1935

Portraying Gentlemen's Clothes of Character, 1933–1934.
Tailored Wear for Gentlemen, Spring/Summer 1935.
Tailor's and Outfitter's Diary, 1937.
When Autumn Comes: Styles for Ladies' Wear, 1933, 1934.

Acknowledgments

I would like to thank Janet Dunham, of Zero Antique Clothes Shop in Newcastle-under-Lyme, for her kindness and help, and for the loan of her many costume magazines.

I also extend my gratitude to the Yale School of Art and Design, Wrexham, Clwyd, for the use of their facilities.